DEDICATION

This book is dedicated to my guru, Sai Baba of Shirdi,
the Saptarishis who send us divine White Light,
Mahaavatar Babaji and His spiritual lineage finding
completion in Guruji Paramhansa Yogananda,
my two little angels Amritaa and Avighno,
my husband Anindya who loves and supports me unconditionally,
my mother and father, who made me what I am today,
my mother-in-law and my father-in-law
whose blessings help me cross over from darkness to light,
and, to people all over the world who seek divine inspiration.

White Light Meditation : Manifest Your Dreams And Aspirations

White Light Meditation : Manifest Your Dreams And Aspirations

CONTENTS

	Acknowledgments	i
1	Introduction	Pg 1
2	Who Am I?	Pg 4
3	The Soul – The One That Dwells Within	Pg 6
4	White Light Meditation: Introduction	Pg 9
5	White Light Meditation: The Process, Dos And Don'ts	Pg 14
6	Seeking Out To The White Light	Pg 22
7	The Key To Happiness	Pg 23
8	Simple Ways To Invite Happiness Into Our Lives	Pg 25
9	The Heart Of Spiritual Living: The Attitude Of Gratitude	Pg 30
10	About The Author	Pg 33

White Light Meditation : Manifest Your Dreams And Aspirations

ACKNOWLEDGMENTS

I am grateful to my Reiki Gurus,
RMT Nemai Nandi & RMT Shanu Singhal, for having imparted to me the knowledge of Reiki healing & of Reiki teaching,
Grand Master Parul Dutta for having brought to my knowledge the realm of spiritual healing,
and, RMT Jayanti Karthikeyan for having inspired me with the selfless spiritual aspects of Reiki.

White Light Meditation : Manifest Your Dreams And Aspirations

White Light Meditation : Manifest Your Dreams And Aspirations

1. INTRODUCTION

All matter consists of energy, energy that is dense, visible and tangible, as well as energy that is light, subtle and invisible. We too are made up of both physical as well as subtle energies. Most of us are unaware of the subtle aspects of our existence that envelope our physical bodies. However, it is a fact that we are not confined within just the physical bodies. Our existence pervades many other energy levels that humans do not sense unless their sensory portals have been opened up through special exercises that stimulate the chakras or subtle energy convergence points located at these portals.

There are some subtle energies, mists, or light that exist everywhere and all around us, and do NOT require any special initiation or attunement to enable humans to access them. *White Light is one such natural divine energy that cleanses and saturates the receiving entity with positivity.*

White light is free and universal. It emanates from the spiritual realm of the universe and comes to anyone, anywhere, no matter what his or her spiritual advancement or awareness or openness might be. For us to access, channelize and contain this light, we only need to intend mentally that we want to do so.

White Light Meditation : Manifest Your Dreams And Aspirations

Doing White Light Meditation every day turns around situations, mends lives and manifests dreams in reality! In white light meditation the wishes of the heart are visualized as thoughts in the mind and infused with the power of the white light.

This book primarily deals with white light meditation. Towards that end, we will begin our discussion identifying who we really are, how we are connected with God through our souls and the significance of listening to the inner voice. Then we will cover the core subject matter, the knowledge of white light meditation, where I shall explain how you can actually live your dreams and manifest your aspirations in real life. Later on, I have also included some notes on how you can bring joy to yourself and to others, how you can experience true happiness or bliss in life through simple acts of generosity and love. I hope you will read, understand, absorb and implement them in your own lives. You will find them under Key to Happiness and Inner Awareness. These are based on my personal experiences and realizations, and I hope you will benefit from them as much as I did! The last chapter throws light on the core attribute of spiritual living - gratitude. I have witnessed many lives transform in so many ways one can hardly imagine, simply by imbibing this one attitude of gratitude.

I would like to share with you how this book came about; I believe a book carrying a spiritual message has to happen just the way this one did-

I had almost finished writing a different book, a novel, when an incessant urge compelled me to shelve it at the point when it was just ten or so pages away from completion, and instead had me start on this one. Honestly speaking, I was surprised to find White Light Meditation had substituted my unfinished novel.

I had conceived the idea of writing a book on white light meditation a long time back. However, I had never really planned or given it a serious thought. So, before I started writing it, I surrendered to higher intelligence and penned down whatever channeled through me. From my previous writing experiences I know that is the way to invite divine grace into my work. And every time I did that in the past, I found it hard to believe that the level of perfection it enjoyed came from me, or rather through me!

In course of writing this book too I did not conjure up the content that could candidly explain the celestial phenomenon of the white light for the beginner, and enlighten him or her with the knowledge of white light meditation. Instead, I surrendered to its grace, and my prayer was heard - words simply poured in and before I knew it, this book was done!

As you read this book, welcome the white light into your life and be open to feeling its divine vibrations. May the sacred energy flowing through this book give you the answers you are looking for and unlock the gateways to untold blessings!

2. WHO AM I?

Each one of us has a name, just as I am Sunetra. But who is the one that dwells within me?

You might have noticed every time you are thinking or trying to take a decision, even as the mind reasons out and justifies why you should take one option, and not the other, there is another faint voice coming from within, sometimes saying 'yes' and sometimes saying 'no' to what your logical mind suggests. That means something within you, a quiet presence, keeps a close watch and wants to guide you every time you are about to take a decision, or an action. Notice that this inner voice is louder and clearer when you are making up your mind on something crucial in life.

Some of you might not be aware of this presence in the rush of daily life. So you sometimes heed and sometimes choose to ignore the soft voice that speaks within our heart. When you ignore it, and choose to go with the practical mind, the inner voice gets suppressed. But that's just for the time being. It keeps playing in the sub-conscience again and again, reminding you who you are, and pointing out the mistake you are about to make. And deep within your heart, you know there's a slight hitch about what you are about to do, though your conscious mind asks you to ignore it. You will hear that voice time and again long after you have moved on against it. It will keep reminding you on and off with a little prick in your heart; for that is its very nature.

Someone within you is aware! It is an integral part of you, and yet you mostly choose to ignore its presence. This someone is on constant vigil. This someone is your soul – a miniscule energy of the Almighty Spirit that came to live on earth as you. It knows when you are wrong, speaks to you through your conscience and guides you to the right path. It always urges you to do what will be good for you in the long run, though it might apparently seem unwise or impractical under the present circumstances. And that is why you might not have agreed with it all the time, out of fear – the fear of losing, of shame and embarrassment, of hardships, or of social pressure. But at times when you did listen, took the right way and set things right, peace was restored in your heart. The little prick within your heart was gone forever, as if a thorn had been plucked out, or a burden had been lifted off your chest, and you felt relieved. If you think about it closely, you will realize that it has happened to you many times. Due to short-sight of the future, and 'feel good is good' nature, most of us tend to choose the logical option, ignoring all inner conflicts.

In the following chapter we shall try to identify the soul within each one of us and discuss the answer to: Should I listen to my mind, or should I listen to my soul? And why?

3. THE SOUL – THE ONE THAT DWELLS WITHIN THE SOUL - THE REAL YOU

Your soul is the core of the entity that is 'you'. It is the indestructible spark of divinity within you. It is the eternal nameless aspect of you that was, is, and always will be. It is your spirit, the nucleus of your existence. It is extremely gentle, subtle, and whispers God's will to you. It always brings God's messages to you because it is always connected with God, the universal power, the source energy of all creation. Thus, through your soul you are always connected with God. Through your soul He guides your wandering mind and signals you what to do, or not to do every single moment of your life! You might or might not be listening because most of the times, the mind overrides the soft whispers of the soul.

The mind is your thinking faculty. It logically analyzes every situation on the basis of information collected by your senses and from your past experiences. The soul, however, has a very different potency and purview. Its cognizance encompasses life beyond time and space. It has access to the very source of all information. It has the power to take the most perfect decision. In any situation, the very first thought that comes to you from within, even before you could think and rationalize, is the voice of your soul.

This is the difference between the soul and the mind. What your mind says is based on limited or incomplete information. What your soul says is based on complete information. Now is the time for you to decide who you will listen to the next time you have to take a decision. Will you listen to the voice of your soul? It is the perfect way to stay connected with God all the time. There is nothing more secure than that! We humans are short-sighted, that is, we do not see the future. So the decisions we take would be based only on our memory of the past and our knowledge of the present. That is why sometimes in life we find that the decisions we took earlier proved to be wrong in course of time. But the soul definitely has a better vantage point, it would always be able to tell right from wrong based on the future possibilities of every decision. Accordingly, it would try to warn you, or encourage you with your choices.

LISTEN! Every time you are confused and don't know what to do, ask your soul. Then carefully listen to the inner voice, that subtle feeling within you that tells you "I should" or, "I should not". It will always guide you in the right direction, help you avoid mistakes and misdoings every step of the way, especially at life's crossroads, so in future, looking back at things, you would not regret.

When you regard the voice of your soul, you heed God's voice, and you will never go wrong or be guilty of doing wrong. It means you have chosen to be in God's grace, and it also means you are bringing divine energy to all those around you. Every thought, word and action then becomes an expression of God's will. You radiate positivity to everyone you interact with, and they sense it! You are accepted and appreciated at large because you radiate positivity, and nothing can outshine that!

Identifying the divine energy within yourself brings you intimately close to It. You are able to perceive that a smaller version of the Almighty power, a micro universe dwells right within you. You can now identify yourself with it. Your awareness gradually widens and ultimately merges into the greater, macro universe. Your consciousness pervades the universe in its entirety! You experience oneness with nature. You identify yourself with its vastness that extends beyond time and space. You realize, after all, you are a speck of celestial energy, a spark of divine light!

This is the ultimate state of existence - when you are one with the universe! Once this state is attained, all pettiness vanishes from your mind, ignorance is invaded by enlightenment and the image of life acquires a much greater stature; as if you are reborn, and now you want to live for a greater purpose.

The following chapter introduces to you the spiritual phenomenon of the White Light and explains the concept, power and uniqueness of White Light Meditation.

4. MAKING THINGS HAPPEN WITH WHITE LIGHT MEDITATION: INTRODUCTION

Every life has a purpose, and every soul has a dream. That is what each one of us has come to manifest on earth. Dr. Martin Luther King Jr. said, "I have a dream!"; his dream changed the face of America, securing justice and equality for all. Everyone has a dream in life. By dream, I mean a wish, an aspiration - a strong yearning to manifest a thought into an accomplishment in life. A dream could be an ambition to become a doctor, a lawyer, or a teacher; a dream could be a desire to see your child healthy, or to see him or her succeed; it could be to reach a certain goal in life, financial, educational, spiritual, or otherwise; it could also be to have a peaceful relationship with someone, or to mend a tormented one; to find someone to share life with; to be able to secure or serve someone the way you have always wanted; to visit someone or, to go on a pilgrimage – it could be anything for that matter.

In order to manifest your dream or aspiration into reality, you must empower it with your will force. Because will force can achieve just about anything! Now, there are two aspects to will force that will enable you to realize your dreams. They are — the divine will, and your individual will.

White light transforms a 'wish' into a 'will'. It empowers your dream with the vital energies essential to bring about the necessary positive changes within you, and around you, to draw all required resources to you, and to smoothly drive you to your target. So basically, it shuffles, cleanses, brings together, connects, harmonizes and organizes resources that are the essential to achieve your dream, and imprints upon it the final seal of divine blessing.

White light meditation is all about infusing the white light into your dreams. It takes care of two things at the same time- nourishing your aspirations with divine blessings, and activating the individual will force within you, thus unlocking your latent power even you were unaware of.

The moment we conceive a dream or think of a plan, in terms of energies it has taken birth already, but resides in the mind as subtle or abstract energy. In order to 'live' the dream we need to concretize it into the physical tangible world. White light meditation aims at empowering the thoughts with the divine energy of the white light, charging you with the vital catalytic force you require to bring your goals to the finishing line.

The White Light:

White light is omnipresent and flows freely in nature. It is accessible to anyone. Most of us do not feel or see it unless we are spiritually aware. But the moment you think of it, whether you realize it or not, the white light comes to you and can be directed to any part of the body simply by <u>intending</u>. However, for manifestation we visualize it at the third eye.

White Light Meditation : Manifest Your Dreams and Aspirations

About White Light Meditation:

White Light Meditation is short, simple and does not need expert guidance, rigorous practice and experience. Once you intend for the white light to flow and shine through you, it will, even though there might not be any physical evidence of the same. The greatest proof of its effectiveness is the happening of the desired changes and the amazing turnaround of situations, persons and events in your life.

White light meditation -

- provides the necessary motivation, the strength of determination, perseverance and endurance to stay focused on your goal throughout the duration of your endeavor;

- opens up options and possibilities, removes doubts, inhibitions and confusions that might have held you back all this time;

- brings clarity of thoughts, authority and firmness of decision;

- removes obstacles and hindrances that might have blocked the way to your goals;

- brings to you the necessary knowledge and resources, even from sources you might not have been aware of until now, finally leading you to completion.

The meditation takes just ten to fifteen quiet minutes every day. It works better if you are mentally relaxed. So it is necessary that you spend the first few minutes of this meditation to calm down mentally and emotionally.

Thinking of what we want, wish, and will comes very naturally to us. This artless nature of the white light meditation makes it come to you spontaneously, and that is exactly how you should approach it.

White light meditation does not take practice to be perfected. Here, I emphasize on the fact that in order to start white light mediation even

White Light Meditation : Manifest Your Dreams And Aspirations

for the first time you do not need the physical presence of a trainer, teacher or a guru. You do not need to get initiated or attuned to the white light energy or to the practice of white light meditation to be able to seek and channelize the white light. A sincere intent to do so is all you need. White light comes to you as soon as you think about it. And that is its uniqueness.

Many of those whom I have instructed about white light meditation have not done any spiritual courses, and have not been initiated or attuned into any other energy fields. Your prior exposure to spirituality does not matter. There is no fear of going wrong since this is an open and spontaneous exercise. The instructions I have given in this book are to serve you as a guide through your meditation. Once you have understood how you should do it, you might want to do it for longer or more often than once a day because the innate nature of this meditation is to calm you down from within. The almost instant positive changes it brings all around you makes you endear the light even more! I know many who practice white light meditation more that once a day due to its flexibility of process and unbelievable benefits.

White Light Meditation brings changes within a week or two, no matter how minute or huge they are. However, some find changes showing sooner, even within a few days. Little processes start here and there, you must keep noticing - people change; their attitude towards you change; situations brighten up; many more options and possibilities appear before you; internally you undergo positive changes; you rediscover yourself and discover your hidden potential; your positive attitude and behavior draw resources towards you in the form of people, money and material. Things start to happen like never before because divine will is at play. All these processes finally get carefully woven together into the fabric of your dream.

It is important to perform white light meditation every day. Regularly re-envisioning your dream in the white light empowers you to carry it out, starting from conception, to planning it out, structuring it realistically, organizing the required resources and finally bringing it to the finishing line.

White Light Meditation : Manifest Your Dreams and Aspirations

Once you have had success with white light meditation, you will be clear about one thing, and that is, a lot goes on up in the sky!

Three important things to remember while practicing white light meditation are:

1. Do it sincerely and patiently, whether you do it for ten minutes or longer.
2. Always meditate upon healthy positive changes. Negative intentions do not work here because the very nature of the white light is pure and divine.
3. Do it with your heart and meditate with love.

Although White Light Meditation is very simple and spontaneous, its effects on life, energies and resources is fast, strong and productive. The incredibly natural approach sometimes makes it difficult to realize the power of this meditation. Mostly, after having done the meditation for a few days, or a week, you get to recognize its manifesting power and what that brings to you. Practice it every day and activate your dormant potential; discover all the hidden treasures you are destined to enjoy.

White Light Meditation forms an integral part of many spiritual, healing and meditation programs. I too include White Light Meditation as a part of my Reiki Courses. In the next chapter you will learn the process of the meditation.

5. WHITE LIGHT MEDITATION: THE PROCESS

1. **Find a quiet place for about twenty minutes**; sit down cross-legged in the lotus position (the picture above shows a woman sitting in lotus position); or sit on a chair if lotus is difficult for you. Now, relax. Bring your focus to you. Make sure you are away from phone calls, alarms, door bells, other devices and any other source of disturbance or distraction during your meditation time.

2. **Close your eyes and focus on your heart** while mentally acknowledging it to be the center of your existence. Appreciate the divine presence of your soul within your heart. Think of your soul as a tiny baby, a divine being dwelling within your heart; ponder upon its subtle presence inside you and mentally intend to send it love and affection. Do not be tensed, and do not worry about anything at this stage. Keep aside your concerns for just a few minutes; tell yourself that you will definitely come back to them in a short while. Ignore time; ignore space. Relax all your muscles and breathe slowly and casually.

3. **Think of something that relaxes you:** Mentally visualize the image of God, or repeat a short spiritual phrase or mantra that comforts you, for example, "Aum", "peace", "Our Father in Heaven", "Our Lady", "Bismillah", "Sairam", the face of your child, of your parent or your Guru – any thought that gives you peace and helps you relax. Note that this thought has no religious significance. It should help you calm down and to gather your consciousness back to you, so you can focus within. While doing so, if you get into a spiritual state of mind, then that is even better for you, though not required for the meditation. Calming down is what is required. Spend two to three minutes with this thought. Be silent; stay relaxed and still. Ignore your surroundings. Listen to the sounds playing within you – listen to your heart beat, the sound of silence in your ears, your breath, blood circulating through the veins, and the like. It is fine if you do not hear any of that; do not get anxious to 'hear'. Just stay with yourself and listen within.

4. **Handling thoughts that come to you during the meditation**: Don't think about anything at this point. Let your worries be where they are. You know you will get back to them after ten minutes. At the same time, do not try too hard not to think. If you get busy worrying about not to think then that will take you away from the purpose of the meditation. So if thoughts come to you, let them come and go. Just observe them like a third person; watch them come, watch them change and merge into other thoughts, watch them go away. Thoughts are usually fragmented and flickering, they do not stay for long. After some time your mind will clear out on its own. It is like a child. If you ask a child not to play with a toy, it will keep thinking of playing. If you let it play, then after a short while it is bored with the toy and ready to let go of it.

Once you are mentally settled in the moment, continue to remain seated quietly, preferably in a spiritual state of mind, and stay still. Linger in that stillness for a little while. Don't get impatient even if you cannot usually stay still for long because you do not have to do that in White Light Meditation. The meditation is all about thinking. You are going to spend the next few minutes thinking about your most desired dreams and aspirations. You are going to imagine your dreams at your third eye, that is, at the center of your forehead, just above the brows. Why at the third eye? You might wonder what is the third eye and what is the use of thinking at the third eye?

We know that the human body is made up of physical tissues at the gross physical level. As I have mentioned briefly in Chapter 1, we have a wide subtle existence enveloping our physical bodies. It comprises of our aura, mental, emotional and spiritual bodies. The energies of all these bodies converge at seven major points within our physical body. These convergence points are called 'chakras' or subtle energy centers. The energies vibrate at different frequencies at the seven chakras and transmit energy to the physical body. If this cycle happens smoothly, we stay and feel healthy. The seven major chakras are neatly aligned along an invisible perpendicular meridian running through the center of the physical body parallel to the spine.

The seven chakras are -

1. Crown chakra at the top of the head,

2. Third-eye chakra at the center of the forehead,

3. Throat chakra at the throat level,

4. Heart chakra at the heart level,

5. Solar-plexus chakra at the stomach level,

6. Sacral chakra just below the belly button, and,

7. Root chakra at the bottom of the spine.

White Light Meditation : Manifest Your Dreams and Aspirations

Each chakra governs a set of mental-emotional-physical processes in the human body. In our discussion we shall try to stay focused at the third eye chakra since it is relevant to white light meditation. Every chakra is associated with a color, a syllable, and, has a separate endocrine gland interacting with it.

The third-eye chakra or brow chakra, as it is popularly known, is Indigo in color and communicates with the pituitary gland in the endocrine system. It controls the brain, the sinuses, the nose, and the face including the eyes. This chakra controls our power of intuition, ideas, imagination, vision and intelligence. It is our window to the spiritual world.

A balanced third eye ensures adequate intelligence, promptness of thoughts, envisioning beyond the present, future planning, healthy upper respiratory tracks and sinuses and strong intuition of the unseen and unknown. Activating this chakra through meditation or other spiritual exercises opens our ability to communicate with higher forces and frequencies of the universe. It strengthens our capacity to predict, prepare and project our thoughts into the future. That is why white light meditation works wonders with our thoughts. Visualizing your dream at the third-eye and empowering or charging it up with the white light brings together all the universal energies - inspiration, will power, resources, health, tenacity, and accomplishment, and actually manifests it in real life.

Now that we know what the third-eye is and why we are meditating at the third-eye, let us come back to **White Light Meditation**…

5. **Imagine there is a circular white light at your Third Eye Chakra located at the center of your forehead.** It is coming to you from the spiritual realm of the universe, from the energy belt that stores positivity. You do not have to actually feel or see the light, just imagine it is there. Because, by its very innate nature, White Light comes to you the moment you think of it. Imagine that the light beam is shining on you, has entered through your

head and gathered at your third eye.

Now visualize your dream within the white light at your forehead. Visualize it happening inside the circular light, like a movie running on a white circular screen. See yourself and all the others involved in the accomplishment of your dream. It shows things actually happening, it portrays future events as they should happen for reaching your goals. See all the things that you have always wanted - health, happiness, success, peace, intimate relationships, affluence; whatever it is that you desire. You are visualizing it all happen at your third eye inside the white light. It could be for you or for others: wellbeing, prosperity, success, career, fame, fortune, family life, marriage, friends, and relationships, anything you aspire for. As you imagine it at your forehead, mentally cover it with a sheet of the divine white light.

You could imagine yourself or others happy, successful, and accomplished in family life, at work, in education, in relationships, in public interactions; if there is any important event that you wish would happen successfully, in a particular way, imagine that event within the white light at your forehead, as if it were actually happening the way you want it to be. If there is disease or an imminent danger in your life, watch the person(s) involved getting healed, rejuvenated, and getting back to normal life, staying healthy, happy and safe.

Continue the visualization for at least ten to fifteen minutes. You can continue longer for as long as you want to. Then slowly open your eyes and feel happy with yourself because you have taken the first step towards manifesting your dream. You have sent a huge dose of divine white light energy, and with it all the essentials required to convert your endeavors into accomplishments.

White Light Meditation : Manifest Your Dreams and Aspirations

The empowerment and positive effects of White Light Meditation on your thoughts and aspirations are unimaginable. Do this meditation every day for a minimum of ten minutes and find out for yourself all the blessings it unlocks for you!

Keep my instructions handy for the first few days. Remember, these are guidelines meant to help you. There are no rigid rules that if not followed stringently would affect the meditation or its manifesting power. The meditation always works provided you do it regularly.

At the end of your meditation, thank the Almighty whole-heartedly for bestowing upon you the many beautiful people and opportunities, big or small, you have in life. Express your gratitude for everything including this meditation. Remember, gratitude is a very powerful virtue. It completes the cycle of exchange of give and take between two entities. Remember to express your gratitude to the Almighty every single day. Realize that to wake up and to find yourself and your loved one(s) intact is also a great blessing from above! And, most importantly, practice white light meditation every day to keep the flow of the divine light on, and to ensure that the progression of your dream continues with equal vigor right up to completion.

If you have doubts or queries, please feel free to email to reikisunetra@gmail.com, or visit my website at www.reikigrace.com.

I would like to share with you an intimate realization, an expression of my spiritual experiences, my perception of the Almighty –

"Everywhere I see there is eternal light, and every place is divine! He is here, and He is out there too - but cherished most within my heart, His shrine, His eternal abode. For here I secure His grace forever!"

DOS and DON'TS of WHITE LIGHT MEDITATION

Who can practice white light meditation?

White Light Meditation can be practiced by anyone irrespective of his or her age, socio-cultural background, nationality, religion, or belief. It is absolutely safe, natural and divine. It is important to remember that white light meditation is a spiritual practice and does not accrue to any religion or sect.

Although I have mentioned earlier, I feel it is worthwhile to reinforce to my readers the fact that in order to start White Light Meditation even for the first time you do not need the physical presence of a trainer, teacher or a guru. You do not need to get specially initiated into the white light meditation or to the white light energy to be able to seek and channelize it through you. A sincere intent to do so is all that is required to bring the light to you. White Light comes to you as soon as you think about it; and that is its uniqueness.

I have gifted White Light Meditation to numerous individuals who have not done any spiritual course as such, and have not been initiated or attuned into any other spiritual energy field. Most of them have noticed amazing changes and turnarounds within a few days of starting White Light Meditation.

Meditating on the White Light during pregnancy, visualizing a normal and healthy conception, pregnancy, delivery and a normal healthy and happy baby can do wonders by nourishing the mother and the foetus with the divine grace of the White Light.

Children who have the maturity to visualize can also meditate with the White Light. I advice children to start the meditation between ages eight and ten years depending upon individual maturity level.

Is there an ideal time or place to practice white light meditation?

White light meditation can be practiced at any hour of the day or at night, and anywhere. However, finding a relatively silent place would be conducive to the meditation process, especially for those new to meditation, since it would help them concentrate.

Note that it is better to meditate at least twenty minutes after a heavy meal. It makes focusing easier. The physiological energies are mostly occupied in digestion right after meals. Besides, the meditation relaxes you so much that you tend to doze off when the stomach is full. On the other hand, meditating on an empty stomach is not a good idea since the mind would naturally crave for food! It is therefore best to do White Light Meditation when you are neither hungry nor too full. Choose a time at least twenty minutes after a meal to two and a half hours after a meal, that is, before you are likely to be hungry again, depending upon how often you need to eat.

7. SEEKING OUT TO THE WHITE LIGHT

In the previous chapters we have discussed most aspects of White Light Meditation. My primary reason for writing this book was to spread the knowledge of the universal presence of the White Light, the untold divine grace it brings to you and its incredible power to manifest your wishes, aspirations and dreams into reality.

I have been practicing White Light Meditation for over a decade now. The open and flexible nature of the meditation permits me to practice it anytime anywhere and in the face of any adversity in life. Besides manifestation, the White Light can bless in many more ways -

You can turn to it for spiritual guidance; for relaxation, especially when you are stressed or overwhelmed with situatoins; for calmness and inner peace and to stay focused in the middle of a busy or confusing state of affairs in life. Mentally seek out to the White Light for direction, for resources, to reinforce confidence and to fortify you from negative influences. Remember, the White Light comes to you the moment you think of it.

8. THE KEY TO HAPPINESS

Happiness is a state of mind. It is the state of mind we are in when we are drenched with positive energy. The more we create positivity within and around us, the more the mind stays in this celebrating state, and the more the joy beams out in all directions to everyone it comes in contact with. While amplifying and projecting joy everywhere the mind attracts similar energy from others too. Ultimately this energy exchange becomes something like a set of mirrors reflecting each other, spreading joy to so many. With the blessings it brings back, the mind sails into ecstasy!

This is exactly how it works. Remember how everything feels great when we feel happy? And all this starts with just one positive thought.

True Happiness or Bliss Comes From Within:

The critical importance of positive thinking cannot be over-emphasized! Actually, that is how happiness is generated within us, by thinking good, and not from external sources. Bliss is found deep inside the individual being, inside the soul - the subtle one that resides within each and every one of us.

"If this HAPPENS then I will be happy, if it DOES NOT happen I will not be happy" is short-lived happiness, or rather a desire or craving for something. True happiness, or bliss, is never subjective. It does not depend upon external conditions.

We think something or someone would make us happy or sad; why should we subject our state of being, our feelings and our precious moments to events that we have no control on? Why not attach our happiness to us alone? –Let the one sitting inside my heart generate happiness for me, the one I can talk to and rely on. It always listens, agrees, comforts, supports and directs me unconditionally. Let us draw happiness from that inner being, the Soul! If we do that, real happiness, lasting and unconditional, will automatically shine forth from within. Our minds will then generate positive and good thoughts only. Good thoughts will automatically lead to good words and to good deeds.

In reality, with most of us, the mind is seldom tuned in with the soul. In order to attach the mind with the soul you need to consciously seek out to the soul; you need to pay attention and listen to its subtle whispers; you need to abide by it. The soul speaks to you at all times. If you were to ask the soul in any situation, "What should I do?", it would have something to tell you. If you would listen and obey, you would avoid many wrong decisions in life. The soul sees beyond time and space. It sees the future and gives advice knowing what fruit every action would bear in the future. Thus Possible mistakes could be turned into untold blessings if you were to listen to that inner voice and follow it without questioning.

The soul tells you something at every step of your life. It is your connection with super-consciousness. Tie a close bond with your soul. Once you are secured, happiness is automatic!

9. SIMPLE WAYS TO INVITE HAPPINESS INTO OUR LIVES

There are so many easy ways to invite positivity and happiness into our lives.

In my spiritual journey I found these Natural Remedies work like magic!-

1. Give Selflessly at Home - Feed Your Visitor:

Is there a crow, a pigeon, a mole, a squirrel, or a deer visiting your backyard?
Every neighborhood will have one or more visitors; I bet yours does too. Does it come to your door-step every day? If so, feed it with inexpensive nuts, biscuits, fruits - food that you could spare. Choose a time of the day when you can do this every day. Invariably, the animal/bird will return the next day, then the next, and then every day after that for food.

You are feeding someone who means nothing to you. You have no emotional attachments with it. Yet you care to provide food for this innocent being. All creatures are made of God energy, and so is this one. And that's the best part. It is a way of worshipping the Creator. But make sure you remember to do it every day. It brings back divine bliss! Providing food is providing the most basic necessity of life, and you have signed in as means to their survival.

2. **Supersede Expectations:**

You interact with a few or a whole lot of people every day; everybody does. Every meeting involves exchange of energies. Other than verbal exchanges, there is an exchange of subtle energies between our aura bodies as well. The Aura is the layer of subtle life energy that envelopes our physical bodies and is always releasing and absorbing energies from its surroundings. Spiritually advanced people have very thick aura well charged with positive energy, even as wide as several meters. The auras of realized souls living in human bodies stretch for kilometers. Thus they say it benefits to even step into the land of a holy man.

Coming back to energy exchanges, whether we talk to others or not, whether we shake hands or not, our auras constantly exchange subtle energies. Some of the energies we receive are positive, but some could be negative as well. Healthy auras are strong enough to repel negative energies from others. People with well energized auras are less likely to get agitated in the company of others even if the latter send out negative vibes. Even infections find it hard to penetrate a healthy aura, while a thin under-nourished aura would allow easy access to germs.

We cannot always control what energy others are sending us consciously or sub-consciously, but we can control ours. No matter what kind of energy you receive, make sure that the energies travelling from you are always positive. Even if it were someone who is not exactly the apple of your eye, try ending the encounter with a "God help you!" kind of a silent prayer. And trust me, it matters! It counts! It blesses the rest of your day! Just make sure you give more than you receive, because that always comes around to you, and might even have gotten amplified by then, so you received much more than you gave!

Some daily examples- tip an honest hard-worker more, hug your mom more than usual, may be make her a hot cup of coffee, or wrap a blanket around her, or help your dad out the way you have never done before. Remember, if you have really helped someone unconditionally, even if it was setting free a trapped ant, you have done your deed for the day! But there is always room for more. So give out positivity to your heart's content! Of course, within your means.

All the above mentioned acts translate to unconditional love; and that's the best way to serve God! Just remember - never bother to brag your selfless deeds, for if you do, they no more remain selfless. You just exchanged them for earning a good name. Instead just enjoy the gladness from having helped in your own little or great ways and cherish it in your heart forever.

3. Don't Forget to Say "I'm Sorry" and "Thank You"

You might think "this is kindergarten stuff!" Well, as silly as it may sound, it's worth revising everyday! Never fail or falter to apologize or express your gratitude whether it is to God, your friend, a relative or anyone else, and when you do, do it right from your heart. It is best to practice true gratitude and true regret than to just say "Thank-you" and "Sorry" merely to show courtesy. Following this rule always reserves a portion of others' blessings for you. And blessings, the purest energies, count more than anything else! Blessings have the power to change the course of one's life. Only blessings can make life as good as it could get by bringing to you the very best of what your destiny holds, and in some cases, even beyond! In that context, when you are practicing White Light Meditation, you are actually blessing your own wishes with divine energy!

Earn all the blessings you can with honesty, sincerity and love.

4. Always be Honest

In many situations, at life's crossroads honesty might be the tougher of two choices, but it's worth the trouble, take my word for it. Unless it is for a greater cause, do not lie. Lying amounts to deceit. Deceit is even more harmful to you than what it did to the other person. Why? You just signed up for misery. Sending out negative energies in the form of deceit, jealously, hatred and anger only invites greater negativity in return. Whereas, sending out positive energies in the form of love, sharing, caring, blessings, help and sacrifice brings back many times more positivity, sometimes even shielding us from destined catastrophes in life.

5. Never Hurt the Soul

Every soul is a part of the Super Soul, that is, every soul is a part of God! So never ever hurt someone. If you think you hurt someone unintentionally, ask for forgiveness as soon as you realize your misdeed. The moment you realize you will repent, and the moment there is remorse, the negativity gets washed away. Once you are aware of your mistake, you will be careful never to let it happen again.

6. Do Your Duty

Well, whether it makes sense or not, whether it feels good or not, even if the beneficiary is not quite the apple of your eye, just do it - do your duty. Ask God to give you strength if it seems difficult. Sometimes we owe someone from the past (even past lives). We better set the books right here so it doesn't get carried forward to later when we are aged or less capable. Nature will have you do your part one way or the other; rather get it done with now than later. Doing your duty also ensures that others will do theirs' towards you when you are at the receiving end.

7. Keep a Broad Mind and an Open Heart

Depending upon the kind of person you are, you will attract similar energies around you, and others will reciprocate with similar energies. Be kind, compassionate and empathetic so you can attract kindness, compassion and empathy in return. Spread love and enjoy being loved back!

8. Think Positive

We manifest our dreams with our positive thoughts. Everything begins as a dream in the subconscious mind, gets organized as conscious thoughts, and gets enacted as events in life. That is how we design our lives within the limits of our destiny.

Think positive, think on, and believe in your heart that is your reality. Dream, think and act good, and so you will be. It doesn't take long for thoughts to materialize, provided the same thoughts prevail over time.

9. SMILE!

Smile to be happy
Smile 'coz it's healthy
Smile so it spreads all around you;
Smile to make a friend
Smile and set the trend
Smile to every living being around you;
Smile to the trees
Smile to honey bees
Smile to the person who found you;
Smile to your brother
And to your step mother
Smile so it's sweet all around you!
Smile at its beauty
Smile when on duty
Smile, smile 'coz it's cool!
Smile when in school
Smile even at nothing like a fool!
So don't forget to SMILE! It's the best gift at no expense!
Smile now, Smile forever!

10. THE HEART OF SPIRITUAL LIVING: THE ATTITUDE OF GRATITUDE

"Always do good to others", "Do unto others as you would have others do unto you"... these are popular sayings that most of us have heard or read before. But do they hold good? If so, let us see how.

The universe runs on the principle of give and take. But energy does not get created or destroyed. It simply changes form. The living world is a physical expression of the divine. Every thought, word, and action, that is, every form of energy that we exude comes back to us in a similar form after gaining momentum through time. So, by the time it comes back to us it is many times more intense than what we had generated.

Our positive thoughts, words and actions come back to us sooner or later in the form of blessings as peace, love, joy, contentment, success, accomplishments and rewards. The opposite holds true as well, and that's where we need to be cautious. If we generate negative thoughts, words or actions like anger, jealousy, hatred, wishing ill, hurting or depriving others, we would get back even stronger negative consequences. Nature always gives back more than it receives. It never keeps anything to itself. So, as we sow, so we reap.

It is also true that the energy we generate attracts the same type of energy from other sources around us. Thus, we design our lives and pack our surroundings with the same kind of energies that we fling towards others. That is precisely how we create our own destiny. Either we attract wish fulfilling resources with our positive attitude, or we repel resources with our negativity. Revisiting White Light Meditation, that is why it is so important to sit and meditate upon your wishes every day, and send all the positive energy you can freely channelize to it in the form of white light.

The Almighty plans in our best interests. Positive thoughts go with God's own thoughts for us and thus get fulfilled soon. Negative thoughts go against God's plans for us. They do get fulfilled at times, or so it seems, precisely in keeping with the free will of the universe, since even God does not impose His will upon us unless we welcome it with an open heart. So He lets us pick our options, right or wrong. However, one would have to face the consequences later on.

To ensure our own wellbeing, it is of fundamental importance that we make conscious efforts to think, speak and do good deeds. And a positive thought is the starting point towards that end. Keeping in mind all that a positive thought can do or trigger, its importance cannot possibly be overemphasized.

The concept of spiritual healing is primarily based on positivity. The entire healing system comprises of building a positive thought pattern, wishing and doing well for oneself as well as for others. As such, the most effectual positive thought that spiritual aspirants work on is *gratitude*. The attitude of gratitude is the basis of a spiritual life; it is at the heart of a spiritually aware being.

The feeling of gratitude makes one realize that everything he or she has is a gift from God and that we are blessed; it teaches one to count the blessings in life and to thank God for being so generous; it takes away ego, the "I" from our idea of life. Thus "I do", "I am", "I will" become "He does", "He is", "He will".

Gratitude is a way of life. It helps us realize we are God's channels doing His will His way in His kingdom on earth. We learn to be grateful for the talents and gifts he has bestowed upon us. We find happiness within our means; from that we learn another great virtue that secures happiness in life… contentment.

White Light Meditation : Manifest Your Dreams And Aspirations

The Attitude of Gratitude forms the core of most spiritual programs, wherein it is either taught as is, or assimilated into the main idea of the programs. The Usui System of Natural Healing or Usui Shiki Ryoho, commonly known as Reiki, is an art of spiritual healing wherein the Universal Life Energy is channelized through attuned individuals who can heal themselves and others with or without touch by intending and letting the energy flow into the recipient from their palms. In Reiki too, the attitude of gratitude is a core component of the healing system. In fact, it is this attitude that shapes an initiated individual into the perfect channel of Reiki.

In order to practice the attitude of gratitude one does not need to be attuned or initiated to it any further than the discussion we had in this chapter. Thank God genuinely every morning after you wake up, after taking a bath, at meal time, thank Him consciously and subconsciously night and day. Think how things could have been without the blessings you have had in life and make the most of them!

God gave us Nature. Nature is full of resources meant for us. Enjoy Nature and give back to others; enjoy the enormous love that comes to you in return.

ABOUT THE AUTHOR

Sunetra Basu is a Spiritual Healer, Traditional Reiki Master Teacher and Writer. She heals, conducts Reiki training programs, provides spiritual guidance via networking websites like Twitter, Facebook, and The Speaking Tree, to mention some. Her spiritual pursuit began in her late teens, and later on led her to the world of healing. She got initiated to the First Degree of the Usui System of Natural Healing, popularly known as Reiki, at the age of twenty-six. Taking to the art of healing and intrigued by its unlimited possibilities, she completed the Second Degree, that is, the advanced healer level in the year 2000.

Sunetra has served as a Reiki Channel for more than twelve years, healing various common ailments, infections, critical diseases, pain, stress and other physical, emotional/mental conditions including depression, heart surgery patients, tumor and malignancy. In 2010, she completed the Master Teacher Degree in Traditional Reiki, in response to an inner call to take up Reiki teaching as her way of life. She teaches Reiki First Degree and Second Degree and plans to launch her Third Degree program in the near future.

Sunetra learnt White Light Meditation in 2000 and has been practicing it ever since. She says, "I seek out to the white light whenever I need divine guidance, seek inner healing, plan an event or pursue a dream." White light meditation forms an integral part of her Reiki programs. She advises everyone including children to practice this simple meditation at any age, and at any stage in life.

This book is the direct result of her inner spiritual calling to spread knowledge of White Light Meditation to the world, to kindle every dream, and to infuse will into every wish.

If you wish to learn more about the author, her healing services and Reiki programs, please visit her website about Reiki, Meditation and Spiritual Guidance at www.reikigrace.com

CPSIA information can be obtained at www.ICGtesting.com
Printed in the USA
LVIW01n1312290118
564424LV00001B/8